Straw Bag
Tin Box
Cloth Suitcase

Three IMMIgrant Voices

Written by Jane Yolen, Marjorie Lotfi,
and Raquel Elizabeth Artiga de Paz

Illustrated by Fotini Tikkou

Reycraft Books
145 Huguenot Street
New Rochelle, NY 10801

reycraftbooks.com

Reycraft Books is a trade imprint and trademark of Newmark Learning, LLC.

Text © Jane Yolen, Marjorie Lotfi, and Raquel Elizabeth Artiga de Paz

Library of Congress Control Number: 2022915649

Hardcover ISBN: 978-1-4788-7589-5
Paperback ISBN: 978-1-4788-7590-1

Printed in Dongguan, China. 8557/0323/19972

Author photos:
Jane Yolen: Courtesy of Heidi E. Y. Stemple;
Marjorie Lotfi: Courtesy of Heshani Sothiraj Eddleston;
Raquel Elizabeth Artiga de Paz: Courtesy of Raquel Elizabeth Artiga de Paz
Illustrator photo: Courtesy of Fotini tikkou

All other images from Shutterstock.

10 9 8 7 6 5 4 3 2 1

First Edition published by Reycraft Books 2023.

Dedications

To the Yolen family and the Morowitz-Berlins, who carry versions of this story in their bones. —JY

To Bahman, Kathryn, and Kamran Lotfi —ML

Quiero dedicar mi parte de este libro a las personas que me han influido a lo largo de la vida. Quisiera incluirlos a todos, pero la lista sería infinita. Con todo mi cariño se la dedico a todos ustedes y les doy las gracias.

A mi padre, Isidro Artiga, y a madre, Rosa De Paz de Artiga.
A mis hermanas y hermano, Laurie Millman, Teresa Córdoba,
Ángel Yañez y Jane Yolen (autora).

¡Muchas gracias a todos! —RA

I want to dedicate my part of this book to the people who have influenced my life's journey. I would like to include everyone but then the list would be endless. With all my love, I give thanks, dedicating it to you.

To my father Isidro Artiga and my mother Rosa De Paz de Artiga.
To my sisters and brother, Laurie Millman, Teresa Córdoba, Angel Yañez, and Jane Yolen (author).

Thank you to everyone! —RA

The rusted old tin lunch box is hidden in a trunk in the attic at Baba's house. Grace is looking for her mother's satin ballet shoes when she notices it and brings it downstairs.

"Momma, why do you still have this?
The paint has come off at the corners!"

Momma's face changes to a look that Grace doesn't see very often.
"Do you really want to know?" Momma asks.

The old straw bag sits by the bedroom door at Nana's house. The room will be Sarah's for this visit, the first time by herself.

"What's in that old bag, Nana?"

Nana takes out a key from a drawer in a bedside table.

"This will be a secret between us, Bubbelah," she says.

Raquel remembers: The small, cheap cloth suitcase stands in the closet, a reminder of their escape, of how little they had in El Salvador. Grinding poverty and the danger of Las Maras Salvatruchas, the gangs.

Raquel had been the youngest of three girls before her brother was born, and then a baby sister. The family hardly talks about that suitcase now.

Sarah puts the key in the brass lock and turns it carefully.
CLICK! The straw bag falls open.
In one part is an apron, three scarves, a pair of boots.
In another, three flowery dresses. The top dress has roses.

"That dress is too small for you, Nana," says Sarah.

"Not my bag," Nana tells her, laughing.
"It belonged to your great-great-grandmother, Manya.
She was old-fashioned before I was old-fashioned.
This rose dress was her party dresses—for weddings, bar mitzvahs."

Raquel remembers: The cloth bag held all they could carry away.
She means away from the once beautiful city of Cojutepeque-
A place where they were so poor, there were weeks with almost
nothing to eat.

Papa had to leave them to find the family a better future.
He borrowed money, emigrated to the North, to America. What
awaited he did not know. He only knew what awaited his wife, his
children—hard work, little food. But one less mouth to feed—his.

"What do you think I kept in this box?" Momma asks.

"A sandwich? Water bottle? An apple?" Grace says.

"Yes, I had packed lunches just like you do, but I don't remember exactly what I put into this box every day. It became my suitcase for a special journey."

Grace was surprised. "It's way too small to be a suitcase!"

"People use all kinds of things as suitcases when they must run away," Momma tells her. "Your Baba knew a man who sewed gold coins into the lining of his coat. Another rolled himself up into a carpet to escape."

Grace notices Momma is holding the lunch box the same way she holds Maman Bozorg's wedding tea glass, like she's afraid it might break.

"Did you have to run away?" Grace asks.

Momma looks sad, remembering. "Not at first. When I was your age, I went to school with my friends, practiced my piano, stuck pink rose petals to my fingernails as nail polish because mother said I was too young for the real thing."

"Can I do that, too?" Grace asks.

"We'll get some roses from the flower shop tomorrow," says Momma.

Great-great-grandmother Manya's second dress is more ordinary, with deep pockets and dandelions.

"For every day," Nana says. "She wore a white apron over it."

"Baking honey cake?" Sarah asks, hoping they can make some.

Nana laughs. "Could be," she says. "It feels like a honey cake day."

Raquel remembers: That first time, Papa was found by the police. He arrived back six months later, a changed man. During the time he had been gone, the family knew nothing of what was happening.

He came home skinnier and with a beard. Only Mama recognized him. He seemed no more than a beloved stranger.

Great-great-grandmother Manya's third dress is black.

"For funerals," Sarah guesses. Nana nods.

"Was that all she had?" Nana smiles.

"Who needed any more in the shtetl?"

"What's a shtetl?" Sarah repeats the odd word carefully.

"A small Jewish town," Nana says. "In Ukraine. Every month or two, fierce groups of Cossacks raided our town. Such a raid was called a pogrom because the tsar—the Russian emperor—wanted them to raid the town. He called the Cossacks his 'fists.'"

So many new words—shtetl, Cossacks, tsar, pogroms.

Momma gets a faraway look in her eyes. "We lived in a country called Iran, the country your Baba is from. At that time, the country had a lot of problems. The king of Iran—called the shah—was very wealthy. But most people were very, very poor. They began to protest, and Grandma and Baba took us to watch the protests."

Raquel remembers how Papa left again.

Mama and the three oldest sisters worked without him.

They sold fruit, vegetables, even a little clothing.

The police found Papa and sent him to Mexico.

"Maybe," Raquel told Mama carefully, "maybe Americanos think everyone who speaks Spanish comes from Mexico, and they are sending him home."

"Were you scared, Momma?" Grace asks.

"I don't remember being afraid at first," Momma replies. "Grandma and Baba said it was important for us to see how ordinary people could change things for the better. But after a while, the protests became more dangerous. I watched tanks roll down our street from my bedroom window. I think then I was scared."

Sarah shivers—she's not sure why. "What did those Cossacks do?"

"They set houses on fire, beat up the Jewish boys . . ."

"Was Great-great-grandmother afraid?"

Nana suddenly laughs. "Not her! She hid her four youngest children in a wagon under straw and drove them all to safety. The older four were already in America."

"Were you in the wagon, Nana?"

Nana laughs again. "Oh, no, dear child, it would be years before I was born."

Raquel remembers: Mama was scared but did not show it.
She had to be strong for the family.
Rosa and Guadalupe were thirteen and twelve. Raquel, ten.
Little Carlos was eight, and baby sister Ruth, four.

The older girls worked hard with Mama to buy food.
"The rest," Mama said, "we can trust to God and our neighbors."
Raquel remembers Mama sighing. "Or wait till Papa comes home."

Later they heard he'd begun to walk alone to the U.S.
For a while he was even lost in the Mexican desert.
And back in El Salvador, the family felt lost without him.

"After one really bad pogrom," Nana says,
"great-great-grandfather Samson told the family
that soon they would go to America.
Great-great-grandmother Manya wasn't happy.
She had chickens and a cow to bring along."

"A cow?" Sarah asks. "In the house?"

"No, of course not," Nana says, "in a barn.
What do they teach in your school?"

"Math," says Sarah. "Reading. Geography."

"And in this geography," Nana asks,
"do they ever teach you where
Ukraine is?"

Raquel remembers: Months later they heard Papa was in America again.
Even though he did not speak English, he managed to get a job on a farm.
He had no documents, so he was very poorly paid.
He worked all day without rest, without time off.
Finally, a Mexican friend who spoke both Spanish and English
helped Papa send what money he had made back to Mama.
Knowing he was alive made them all stronger.

Momma touches the little tin box. Her voice gets soft.
"The government announced a curfew. That meant after a certain time of night, people weren't allowed out of their houses."

She speaks quietly, as if—even now—she's afraid of being overheard. "Some nights I could see people in flowing white robes defying curfew. Our neighbor was one of them, the bravest man I knew. But it became less and less safe for any of us to go out, especially Grandma because she's American, even to the corner shop for fruit, or to the bakers for thick slabs of barbari or the paper-like lavash."

"One day, Baba came home in the middle of a workday, something that had never happened before. He said the airports were shutting that night. He said we had to leave. Right then. Right away."

Nana whispers, "A new pogrom began, the worst ever.
Houses were set on fire, cows stolen, chickens killed.
Everyone ran to the woods. It was dark. No moon.
The rabbi whispered prayers for their safety. When the Cossacks
left, Great-Great-Grandfather said, 'Now we leave Ekaterinoslav.'"

"Did they catch a plane, Nana?"

"No planes then, not like today's planes. The family and their
neighbors walked almost twenty miles, staying off the roads, till
they came to a train station."

"Did they take the train to America?"

"Gevalt! Child," Nana says, "your geography needs work."

Raquel remembers: The gangs learned of the money Papa sent.
They demanded it for themselves, or they would kidnap us girls.
They had done that and worse before in towns nearby.

And then, a miracle. A letter from Papa.

Because of the eleven years he had tried to get to America,
because of abuse he had suffered on the farm,
he was eligible for a visa, able to work towards citizenship.
Plus his family could all come, too. To America!

Momma says softly, "Grandma put on her chador for going out. We drove through a terrible riot in the streets, and fires along the sides of the road. People were shouting and waving flags. There was the rumble of trucks and tanks. Baba wasn't allowed to come inside the airport with us."

"As we went through the checkpoints, Uncle Kamran and I did as much of the talking as possible because Grandma spoke Farsi with an American accent. We didn't want her to get into trouble. And then we finally boarded the airplane."

Mama seems to think a minute. "We'd been on lots of planes together, but this flight was different. All the seats were occupied. The pilot announced that the radar equipment, other instruments, had been taken off the plane to stop anyone from leaving. 'But we will go anyway,' he said. More people got on."

"Where did they all sit?" Grace thinks about the one plane she has been on. It wasn't allowed to leave till everyone was buckled up in their seats.

"They stood in the aisles," Momma tells her. "When there was no more room, the doors were shut, the plane took off."

Grace worries, even though she knows it turned out okay.

"So," Nana says, "the train brought them to a big boat."

"And then they came to America?" Sarah is anxious.

"Not everyone," Nana says. "Not right away. A doctor examined them all for lice and fleas. He looked at their skin for sores, their eyes for redness, their throats. They had to be healthy to get on the ship."

"And then . . . ?" Sarah is worried about her great-great-great-family, even though she's pretty sure she knows how it turns out.

Raquel remembers: The family happiness quickly turned sour.
Rosa, no longer a child at 22, could not be included.
She had to stay behind in El Salvador, that dangerous place.

How could they bear the separation? How could she?

She could stay with aunts and uncles in El Salvador.
She kept the two little dogs for company.

But Papa was waiting—and they had not seen him in so many years.
They promised Rosa she would get to America someday soon.

Raquel remembers: They did not know what awaited in America.
They heard that Massachusetts, where they were going,
was not warm. Not like El Salvador. Their soft suitcase was packed
with only a few pieces of clothing each. And how would they find
Papa in cold Massachusetts? None of them knew English.

Suddenly, their plane was grounded for a day and a night.
There was no food. No one could leave.
Raquel thought: Is it gangs? Or has America shut its borders?

Nana says sadly, "Some of the neighbors from Ekaterinoslav had lice or fleas or sores or coughs or runny noses. They were not allowed to get on the boat. Meanwhile, their sisters or brothers, mothers or fathers sailed off to America without them."

Sarah shudders, imagining sailing off without Mama or Dada or her little brother. Or having to stay behind by herself.

She isn't sure which would be worse.

Momma's eyes seem to sparkle. Grace is not sure if it is tears or excitement.

Momma says, "The next time the pilot spoke he told us we were flying over Germany. Everyone on the plane cheered, thinking we were safe, but then he reminded us that we had no radar. It had been taken off of the plane. He said landing was going to be the most dangerous time. Ground control didn't know we were coming. Without instruments there was no way to warn them. 'We're going to have to pick a runway and land on it,' he said."

Grace held her breath and whispered a quick prayer. Just as Momma must have done on the plane.

"We landed safely, then we got off the plane,"
Momma tells Grace. "I was gripping the tin
lunch box so hard, I had the print of the handle
on my hand for the rest of the day.
I slept with the box for the next few nights,
a reminder of how far we'd come,
how far we still had to go."

Nana continues. "It took many days till they reached America. Great-great-grandmother Manya pointed to the Statue of Liberty, itself a new immigrant, only twenty years old."

"And the straw bag?" Sarah asks.

"Great-great-grandmother held it tightly in her hand."

Raquel remembers: None of the family slept on the plane. They were exhausted, frightened, hungry. But still they did not sleep. The very next morning, they were told the plane could fly.

They flew north. And when they landed, there was Papa. He looked old but happy. And an uncle from Boston, who welcomed them to his home.

Quickly, Nana tells Sarah the rest. "Cousins already living in America met them, then took them to Connecticut, a name none of them—except the two youngest boys—were ever able to pronounce successfully. And there was the rest of the family: their eldest brother, the three older girls who had already learned to speak English, how to cook American foods like pancakes, which were blintzes except not rolled. They had learned to dance the Charleston, listen to the radio, watch moving pictures."

Raquel remembers that the next day they left by bus for western Massachusetts, where Papa worked. He had rented a room for them. Every night bugs crawled over their faces. There was only one bathroom for all the people in the house.

But eventually, after a year, a neighbor took pity on them, rented them a clean apartment. Raquel began to work on a nearby farm. She worked from 2 p.m. in the afternoon till 2 a.m. at night. And no complaints.

"Then on a different plane, one with seats and radar, we flew to America, flew halfway across America," Momma says. Now she is smiling.

"But did Baba ever get there?" Grace asks, even though she sees him almost every day now.

"Grandma and Uncle Kamran and I waited in Ohio for Baba to come out of Iran. We worried constantly, Grandma the most. We worried he was in danger. But then he telephoned and said he was coming to join us. And when he finally arrived the next year to Ohio, we drove the rest of the way across country and started our lives again in California. It wasn't easy, starting all over again, but you'd never know that now."

"We have a good life now," Momma says. "Though sometimes I wonder what life would be like if we hadn't been forced to leave. And your Baba still dreams in Farsi! I've never been back to Iran, but every time I see the lunch box, I remember the treasures I carried in it—stones and notebooks, petals from the garden—all memories of home, the very things you can now carry in it, too."

"Manya always remembered Ekaterinoslav, the chickens, the cows, their good neighbors," Nana says. "After a while, she forgot the Cossacks, except in her dreams. She kept the straw bag in her bedroom, behind the door, ready to leave for home, for her cow and those chickens, back to Ukraine, if ever the Cossacks came to America. Though in all the years, she never went back, until it was finally too late to go."

"It's your memory bag, Nana," Sarah says. "We made them in school."

"And now it's yours," Nana replies.

Raquel remembers: A Colombian woman, a social worker, took her to the Center for New Americans to study English.

In El Salvador, Raquel had many dreams. Being a doctor, a teacher. She even wanted to own a beauty salon. But in America, she decided to study nursing. "It's an honor to be at the moment of birth, or to hold the hand of a dying patient," she says.

Every day Raquel works to become a citizen. She opens the closet and on the floor, in the back, is the cloth suitcase. Once it held only a few pieces of clothing and the family's dreams. "What we have now," she says, "is too big to fit in it. But I would take it back to El Salvador in a minute to bring Rosa here."

About the real families in this book

All three of these stories are fictionalized accounts based on how our families came to America. Our families were fleeing oppression, revolutions, gang violence, possible death. Our stories sound very much the same, though they are generations apart.

Jane

Jane's family on both sides came over to America in the early 1900s from Ukraine (the Yolens), and Latvia (the Morowitz-Berlins). But this telling is much more directly from the experience of the Yolens. The way in which they left—redheaded Manya driving children in the cart, the straw bag—are stories the Yolens tell. That family consisted of mother, father and eight children who, when they came to America (in three different stages, actually), consisted of four girls and four boys, from the oldest boy, 27, then three girls in their late teens, then a boy 10, a girl 9, Jane's father 7, and the youngest boy 6.

They were running from the devastation of the pogroms, those constant raids by Cossacks who were in the pay of the last Russian tsar. That tsar was overthrown and executed with his entire family in 1917, the year the Russian Revolution began. By then the Yolens and Morowitz-Berlins were settled in America. But Manya's straw bag always waited, fully packed, by her bedroom door—just in case they had to make another quick flight from terror.

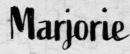

Marjorie

Marjorie was born in New Orleans but moved to Iran with her American mother and Persian father as an infant. She had a very happy and ordinary childhood in Tehran until the Iranian Revolution forced her family to flee to the US in 1978–79. During this time, the shah of Iran was overthrown and 52 Americans were taken hostage in the U.S. embassy in Tehran. As in the story, Marjorie, her mother, Kathryn, and her brother, Kamran, waited as long as possible before leaving. They then lived with family in Ohio until her father, Bahman, got out the following year. Once reunited, the whole family moved first to California and later to Maryland, the place that—even though she lives now in Scotland with her children—she still thinks of as home.

Marjorie works with immigrant groups. She and Jane met because of their mutual interest in writing poetry and decided to write a book together about how their families came to America, once they realized how many of the same sort of things had happened to each of them.

Raquel

The story told here by Raquel is from more recent times. Raquel's family was separated for eleven years, living in poverty, as their Papa tried desperately to raise enough money as a farmworker in America to keep them safe and bring them legally across the border. Even threatened by gang violence, the girls, their mother, and young brother managed to stay alive. Finally, because of the brutality Papa de Paz had suffered at a farm, he was given a coveted visa so he could bring over his wife and four of their five children. (By then, the fifth—and oldest—child, Rosa, was by American visa rules too old to be considered a child and would need to get her own visa and make her own way, asking for asylum by herself. But Rosa has been too afraid to make the trip.)

Raquel is learning English, working as a caretaker with people in their own homes, and singing in a chorus. She and Jane met at the Center for New Americans, and, with the help of translator Laurie Millman (head of the center), they worked on her part of this book together.

Jane Yolen is the author of well over 400 published books, including *Owl Moon* and the *How Do Dinosaurs* books. Her count is heading towards 500 in a few years. She has six honorary doctorates for her body of work. And she writes a poem a day, which she sends out to subscribers. She was the one who initiated *Straw Bag, Tin Box, Cloth Suitcase* and got the other authors to come along.

REYCRAFT BOOKS 2023

Marjorie Lotfi is an Iranian-American who has lived in the United Kingdom for over 20 years. Her first collection of poetry, *The Wrong Person To Ask*, was published in 2023. Marjorie is a founder and director of Open Book, a charity that supports over 1,200 reading and creative writing sessions each year across Scotland, including in prisons, shelters, and with refugee and migrant groups. In her spare time, Marjorie is the chair of the board of trustees for StAnza, Scotland's International Poetry Festival, and an editor of *New Writing Scotland*.

REYCRAFT BOOKS 2023

Raquel Elizabeth Artiga de Paz was born in El Salvador, in the city of Cojutepeque. Although happy that she was able to meet her father again, she never ceases to miss her older sister, who had to stay behind in El Salvador. Thanks to the director of the Center for New Americans, Laurie Millman, Raquel is now a little closer to her great dream of becoming a nurse. Her greatest joy is her daughter, Emily Raquel Artiga.

REYCRAFT BOOKS 2023

Fotini Tikkou is an illustrator and ceramic artist based in Athens, Greece. She studied painting at the Athens School of Fine Arts. Her work includes children's books, editorial illustrations, book covers, art licensing, pattern design, and ceramics.

REYCRAFT BOOKS 2023